Biophilia

Nature and Human Nature

DENNIS CORCORAN

Biophilia
Copyright © 2025 by Dennis Corcoran

ISBN: 979-8993582016 (hc)
ISBN: 979-8993344898 (sc)
ISBN: 979-8993582009 (e)

The views expressed in this book are solely those of the author and reflect the author's own perspectives and experiences.

Dennis Corcoran
owlsheadspirit@gmail.com
www.owlsheadspiritllc.com

Table of Contents

PREFACE

Biophilia, derived from the Greek words for "life" and "love, suggests that humans have an inborn tendency to connect with nature and other living things.

When I pay attention to nature, awareness of my surroundings flourishes, connecting nature with emotions, events, visual stimulation, and interaction. This collection of poetry titled "Biophilia", is written in a combination of free verse and formal verse reflecting personal life experience and observations regarding our environment, and how we interact with it… Nature and Human Nature.

Dennis Corcoran

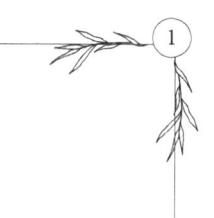

Altitudes

Freedom breathes with nature,
Gazing up at crested peaks.
The sober face gallantly beams;
Windswept clouds billow,
A backdrop, oh so sweet.

The test against my will and power;
A force too great to know by name.
The earth pushed skyward
From a time I have no picture of,
But this I see so vivid, so real.

I cast myself to endear
My curious flight ahead
Not for the unprepared
As experience has taught, I venture upward,
Mentally and physically launched.

At the end, one small step
To stand on top, high in altitude.
Proud, if only for myself.
Pensive for the moment
As the freedom of nature breathes with me.

Biophilia: Nature and Human Nature

Dennis Corcoran

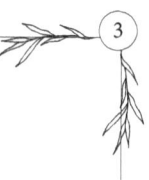

The Ancient Foundation

In my solid place on earth,
The weather knows no quick demise.
I breathe the air without a stir,
And whisper words through my disguise.

Gazing through my naked eyes,
The wind and rain can't penetrate.
The snowfall comes and buries me,
My cover through the winter state.

'Til the sun of spring reveals,
The earth that I recall.
And nature seems to glow once more,
With radiance I don't feel at all.

I am mighty and I am ancient,
No doubt, I'll outlive you all.
I won't miss you when you're gone.
But while on earth, I'll hear your call.

Use my strength and stamina,
And your body will be kind.
Use my cool and solid will,
Medicine for a grounded mind.

And when you need to feed your soul,
Close your eyes and think of me.
Laying solid on the ground,
A rock for all eternity.

The rock lives on beyond our day.
A symbol to me and to you.
Don't give up, it seems to say,
Think of all that I've been through.

Biophilia: Nature and Human Nature

Dennis Corcoran

Arachnid – The Superhero

Hundreds of millions of years in the past,
Spiders existed and continue to last.
The web they spin still captures their prey,
While the site of one will scare humans away.

To be caught in a web that would not let you free,
Only their prey knows how that would be.
The insect brain may not comprehend,
The spiders' next meal means this is the end.

There's also the sting that scares us away,
A black widow bite would ruin the day.
The widow spider with a venomous profile,
Inflicting great pain that would stay for a while,

So fearsome this web-spinning creature became,
It earned Superhero status with the Spiderman name.
With powers that only real spiders display.
Spiderman casts webs chasing villains away.

The spider is the real Superhero it seems,
Surviving the Ice Age, Asteroids and other extremes.
Unlike Spiderman, arachnid is real,
Imperishable existence makes the spider surreal.

So let us give credit where credit is due,
We can't imagine what the spiders been through.
Surviving all Mother Nature has cast,
From hundreds of millions of years in the past.

Dennis Corcoran

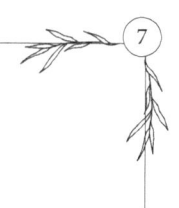

The Calm After The Storm

Winds pick up, dark clouds appear, born beneath blue skies.
Heat and moisture clash above, the forecast no surprise.
Rumbling thunder, flashing light, frightens ears and eyes.
Sheltering to shield the fear, a lightning bolt could mean demise.

Huddled around a candle, the power has shut down.
Heavy raindrops beat the glass, darkness all around.
Anxious dogs and scaredy cats, nowhere to be found.
Hiding from the thunderclap, until they hear no sound.

Thunder at a distance, clouds move slowly by,
Pounding raindrops soften, glimpses of blue sky.
The outage now corrected, from power gone awry.
The worst of it now over, the calm and peace imply.

Sun shines through, the storm has passed, quickly as it came,
The anxious dog and scaredy cat return when called by name.
Candles snuffed, lights back on, things are back the same.
Mother Nature struck again, reminders of her fame.

Dennis Corcoran

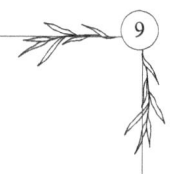

Come Back To The River

A leaf floated by as I watched from a rock at the river's edge.
I paused before casting my line.
Curled up on the edges, the leaf glided freely as the river moved along.
Soon, it was out of sight.
What tree did it fall from? Where would that leaf end up?

Without the river, the journey would be short,
Sailing with the breeze from the tree it fell from,
Spiraling down to the ground.
But it was the flow of the river that took it far from the tree.
It was the river, with all its liquid volume and force.

Forming from the rain, snowmelt and springs,
Gathering and flowing as a stream from higher ground,
Carving a path, as gravity pulls it to lower ground.
The stream collects and flows,
Continuing on the path of least resistance.

The stream becomes wider and deeper,
It is now a river seeking a destination.
Passing me by with a gentle soothing rumble,
I see a break in the surface, a fish it must be.
My mind at ease, I return to the task of casting my line.

. . . . .

If a fish should bite, that would be nice.
If I catch one again, that would be twice.
If I catch nothing at all, that would still be OK.
I'll come back to the river on some other day.

Dennis Corcoran

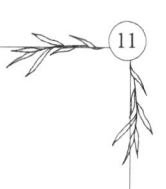

The Depth Of Your Roots

So much to learn from the depth of your roots
Firmly planted for a life on your own
Fueled by soil and sun, and oh that rain
Traveling up your veins, reaching for the sky

Here for a little while giving beauty to the earth
Minding your own business, doing your job
Telling us when the wind moves
And shading us from the sun

Growing tall, like a statue
But so real with your graceful limbs
Reaching out like an angel's wings
To the heavens above with your purpose

You sprout your leaves with all your might
And then lay them down in a vibrant cast of color
Reminding us that the seasons change
And the years go by, one at a time

And then you fall
We are saddened by your demise
But nature knows you will rise again
With a new seed firmly rooted in the ground

Say good morning to the sun and the rain
So much to learn from the depth of your roots

Dennis Corcoran

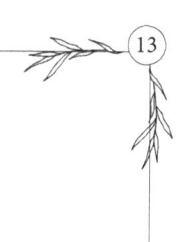

The Fly Ball

Standing in the open field, the sun shines brightly on my head.
The cap I wear, a hopeful shield, to shade my eyes instead.
Ready for the pitcher's best, the outcome never known.
The batter steps up for his test, swinging, all alone.

Thinking of our pitcher's speed, hoping for a strike,
A hit could put them in the lead, don't throw a pitch you think he'll like.
The wind-up and the pitch is free, the batter swings, I hear the crack,
A fly ball hit, it's up to me, I'm back around the warning track.

Soaring high the ball's in sight, I think I've got the line.
The other fielder thinks he might, but I know the ball is mine.
Just then I feel I've hit a truck, my legs fall out from under.
The other fielder and I have struck, a crash that boomed like thunder.

The two of us, down from our fall, hiding heads in shame,
We didn't call out for the ball, and now we've lost the game.
That's the way it goes, coach said, next time you will see,
If you want an out instead, call for it with certainty.

Dennis Corcoran

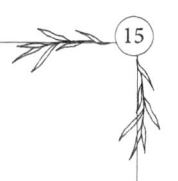

The Flying Kind

As a bird, I see myself soaring over the river, playing with the
wind freely,
like you would expect. When the sun shows itself so early in the day,
I see myself searching for a meal, my eyes piercing through the still
water below.

Diving with precision, I plunge, resurfacing with a purchase, no charge,
just a well-earned meal to last until the next dive.

As the earth continues to orbit our great glowing star, a few
clouds float by,
reflecting on the river below. I continue to frolic in the wind,
trouble free.

The sun begins to fade, and my wings grow weary.
Returning to my nest, I now see life below the trees. I see my friend the
red fox, scurrying around with her nose to the ground in search of her
own fuel for survival.
I see all of those ground creatures that must envy my freedom to fly:

Here, just like the day before,
All I need for my next day.
It may seem an endless chore,
Surviving life in such a way.

My little ones will need it too,
I do my best to keep them fed.
No need for help that comes from you,
I live on Nature's path instead.

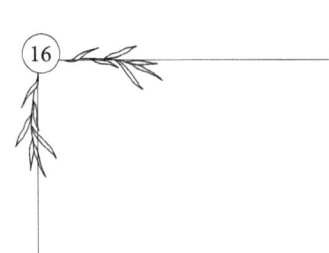

I soar the sky at my own pace,
With wings that set me free.
My home, a simple resting place,
The nest that sits upon a tree.

My simple life, a feathered friend,
Imagined in my mind.
Even if it's just pretend…
If I was born the flying kind.

Dennis Corcoran

Dennis Corcoran

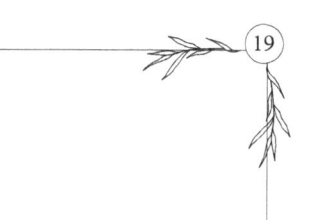

Forgotten Song

Alone in my thoughts, my guitar and my pick,
Searching for sounds to make a song stick.
A song I'm sure that I have not heard,
Notes and chords that have never occurred.

No need for words, with sound so clear,
Stumbling on music so soothing to hear.
Sounds that somehow came from me,
Music as I hoped it could be.

I couldn't stop and continued to play,
Where it came from, I cannot say.
Sounds that mattered, if only to me,
Music the way I like it to be.

Words to this song left untold,
Imagination let the story unfold.
Playing along making music for free.
Music the way I know it can be.

My guitar and pick set back on the stand,
Leaving behind that music not planned.
The forgotten song, the music set free,
A moment in time was the song it would be.

Dennis Corcoran

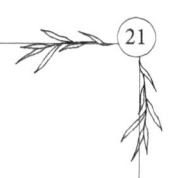

The Generals Charge!

The men hung back, anxious to see,
While officers paced, it didn't look good.
The treacherous mission confronting me,
Seemed perilous from the place I stood.

Wavering indecisively,
I shrugged without a stand.
Like I've felt so frequently,
I stood in fright with no command.

My rank should rest the soldier's mind,
And squash these harsh anxieties.
The choice I make cannot be blind,
To face an enemy set to seize.

Suddenly, the choice was clear,
And action was required.
Reflex took the place of fear,
We charged before they fired.

Their courage raged with heart and soul,
Fearless acts to stand their ground.
The battle won they met their goal,
With pride, I led them homeward bound.

And now when thoughts provoke my mind,
The charge comes back to me.
Results from which I am defined,
Come from instincts I can't see.

Dennis Corcoran

The Grapes

Growing on woody vines in orchards for thousands of years,
Cultivated best with sunlight and heat.
A naturally sweet and healthy fruit,
A good source of vitamin C and fiber.

A fruit that has been a symbol of abundance and celebration.
Featured in colors of red, green and blue-black.

And then of course, there is the wine.
Waiting around for just the right time,
For a pour in the glass and a scent to define,
To sip and to savor when you sit down to dine.

What tempts me most is a red Cabernet.
Robust, full-bodied, let it linger, they say.
Others may like a buttery, smooth Chardonnay.
I might too, it depends on the day.

I've also been known to enjoy a red Zin.
Just look for a bottle in the Zinfandel bin.
At the end of the day, a nice way to begin.
A bolder taste that explodes from within.

Whatever the case may be.
California, France or Italy.
A wine for you and a wine for me.
Swirl and sip, how it's meant to be.

Dennis Corcoran

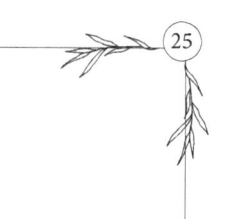

His Dog

Slurping water from the bowl, drooling, not a care,
Her comfort lies within these walls.
And the master will return, like always.
Rest assured and rest easy all day long, waiting…

Waiting for that certain sound,
Familiar to her ears.
The Chevy sound that brings him home,
The engine purr, distinct from all others.

Right again, that same door slamming,
Followed by the master's steps,
Anticipating the twist of the doorknob,
The big event each day.

Jumping with delight, a daily celebration,
Things in order now.
Peace and harmony, and the kin she knows.
Food will follow, she is sure.

The leash is next.
The buckle clicks, her heart pounds.
Frolicking, sniffing, exploring the world so open.
Slowing to a walking pace, panting.

Then the return, the comforts of the den.
More water, sleep, dreams…
Running through pastures, chasing rabbits,
Master at my side.

Biophilia: Nature and Human Nature

Gone again, the twisting knob,
That sad old Chevy sound.
But she knows just when to listen,
For that happy Chevy sound.

Dennis Corcoran

Dennis Corcoran

Its Certain Presence

The fog rolled in, suspended in the atmosphere, hanging at the surface of the lake.
The picture in my mind of blue sky and sunshine from the previous day diminished.
A cool thick mist filled the air and a silvery gray wall formed eerily at the shoreline behind trees with dark shadowy branches and dull green leaves.
The earth was hauntingly still.

Looking out through the glass of the lakefront cottage, there was no lake to be seen, just the mystery of its' certain presence, provoking serenity and arousing a sense of calm to my inner thoughts and emotions. As the gloomy day came to an end, sunset was lost, sensed by the passing of time.

No moon, no stars, just darkness. Deprivation of light encouraged deep sleep.
Cryptic dreams appeared matching the mystery of the seductive cover of ghostly fog.

After sleep a new day would approach. Would it be Sunshine capturing the sharp contrast as my eyes feast upon the images across the lake of towering flushed trees sandwiched between infinite blue skies and the rippling waves, or would there be the mysterious fog, leaving me only to imagine the certain presence of the lake?

Say hello to fog today,
It came without a word.
Hiding natures gifts at bay,
With views severely blurred.

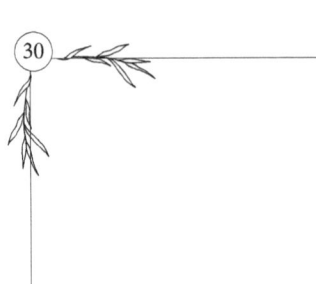

Hidden by the cover of hazy mist,
Its certain presence not in sight.
The lake to view could not exist.
Until the sun shows rays of light.

If the sun should show its face,
The fog would surely disappear.
Blue skies and sun to take its place,
The lake out front now crystal clear.

Dennis Corcoran

Dennis Corcoran

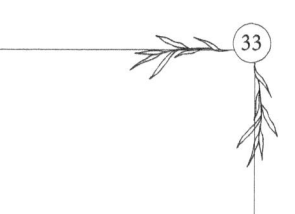

The Last One Standing

To the last one that stands
Among our closest friends,
Let us shake each other's hands,
Knowing life ahead depends....

The life behind that we've all known,
The joy, the loss, the laughs and such,
A blessing so results have shown,
With friends that mean so much.

The time we've spent, short or long,'
Living close, or far away,
Bonds not broken, built so strong,
Proven from our own display.

Our time will pass one by one,
Recalling memories from our past
For now there's still more time for fun,
Until the one left standing last.

To the last one standing...
Among our little group of friends,
Thanks for carrying the weight.
Until then,
What shall we do now?!

Dennis Corcoran

Little Leaguer

Who knew the times we had ahead,
That first day of little league ball.
The first bad pitch, you swung instead,
And a strikeout from the umps bad call.

Who knew the ups and downs we'd share,
From the games you'd win and lose.
When you reached home plate with time to spare,
Or the long ride home from the bad game blues.

I wouldn't trade it, not at all,
The memories stick like glue.
Now there's more with high school ball,
A pleasure still from watching you.

The dream is ours, you may not know,
I see it in your eyes so eager.
But if it ends on your last throw,
I'll be there for my little leaguer.

Dennis Corcoran

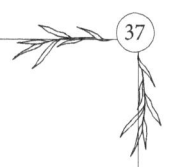

Love Is The Champion

Our world… So full of unique human minds, bodies and souls.
Each one of us so distinct in the way we think, the way we look,
The way we speak, and the way we are.

Born to this world with energy to live, in the limited time we have.
Born with a desire to be meaningful
In a world full of minds that want the same thing.
Who am I? Why am I here? What can I do to make a difference?
Unlike other creatures born to nature with the instinct to eat
and survive,
As humans, we want more. We want to make a difference.
How can my legacy live beyond my years?
Our mind fuels creativity, ingenuity and a competitive spirit.
We think, we project, we create and we achieve.
Always striving for more.

We pride ourselves with how we impress.
We honor those who have impressed us the most.
With that honor comes respect, and sometimes wealth…
Wealth in a material world, obtained by few.

Happiness is different.
Happiness evolves from nature and human nature.
It is only with the chance of nature that we find love.
That love, such a lucky thing, is the ultimate reward.
That love, greater than all things collected in the material world.

Love is available to everyone, it brings out our best.
When all is said and done, Love is the champion.

Biophilia: Nature and Human Nature

Dennis Corcoran

Mad March

The gray sky dulls the skin of the winter trees.
The brightness of the Spring leaves is yet to come.
It is the unpredictable month of March in this place.

The river below is masked under a dark sky,
avoiding the reflection of a hidden sun.
Rainfall bounces gently off the surface,
creating tiny circling ripples.

The gentle sound of rain on the roof above
fluctuates with the wind, soothing to the mind and soul.
The awesome wonder is not in our control,
for tomorrow could bring a bright sun
reflecting a warm radiance,
on the same cold, dull river from the night before.

March arrives, the third month of the year,
The weather is hard to explain.
The transition from Winter to Spring is now here,
It could be snow or it could be rain.

Waking each morning to a brand-new day,
Mother Nature decides on clouds or sun.
No matter your thoughts she will have it her way,
And soon, another day will be done.

Tomorrow will come and whatever the view,
We'll just have to wait and then see.
The sky could be gray or the sky could be blue,
It's March, who knows what it will be?

Dennis Corcoran

The Magic Of Nature

The water was still, like a mirror.
Puffy white clouds were reflecting upon it,
Branches of tall pines could be defined with precision.
The vibrant blue of the sky,
The bright white of the clouds
And the deep green of the pine trees
Were plain to see looking up or down.

Gazing across the river
A fish reaches the surface,
Seeking a meal from a floating fly.
Tiny ripples spread in a circular motion.
Soon there is calm again.

The Eagle soars above purposefully,
Powerful wings flapping with grace.
Pausing at times with an upward draft.
Eyes piercing through the water below.
A familiar shadow appears.
The eagle descends convincingly,
Talons extended, aiming for the shadow.
The unsuspecting fish is plucked from the water.
The Eagle returns to flight, meal in hand.

From the fly to the fish to the Eagle,
In the magic of nature.

Dennis Corcoran

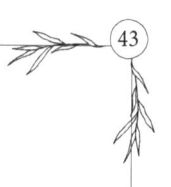

Me & My Guitar

Sometimes, in place of you is my steel guitar,
trying to fill a void in my heart and my soul.
It does a pretty good job.

It stimulates my mind and brings some joy
when I feel I'm hitting it right.
It sits there in a stand,
waiting patiently for me to give it some attention.

When I capture the moment,
I only hope I can satisfy my steel guitar
by making it sing with sweet music.
I'm not the best, but I don't stop trying.

My guitar hangs in there with me like a loyal pet dog
waiting to be fed, or taken for a walk.
My guitar never complains.
It waits with open strings, waiting to be picked.
I am equally loyal to my guitar.
It stands proud in my view,
and I approach it as often as I can.

We are not perfect together.
My guitar might be happier with more attention,
like in front of a captured audience.
I would certainly be happier if I could satisfy that desire.

We don't expect too much,
but when we connect, it's a good thing.
I won't surrender my guitar, and it won't surrender me.
We make good music together.

Biophilia: Nature and Human Nature

Dennis Corcoran

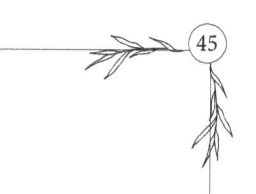

My Silver Lining

Hours and days slide by as our Earth stands still for a moment
One small grain of orbital mass circling around the great sun

With God's famous human life, struck by Nature's ill command
Accepting a pandemic and adjusting, with a will to live on

So many small lives, overwhelmed with questions of why
Each miraculous mind, trying to comprehend
And within that world of miracles
There is one particular mind, our own

Our own brave mind, looking for the other side
Fending off uncertainty and fear; hopeful
Hopeful to grab the slices of joy our Nature longs to provide
And one man's story surfacing in his thoughts

I stand still in time unable to change what is
But within the silence, there is a voice proclaiming
Our tiny lives erupt with uncanny timing
This is my time and this is what I see

Underneath the pain, not so unique to me
There is a light, as bright as it can be
I am guided to that light, it draws me near
It warms my heart and calms my fear

It circles my mind and captures my soul
A slice of joy that renders me whole
So lucky to be here with uncanny timing
And the friends that are my Silver Lining

Biophilia: Nature and Human Nature

Dennis Corcoran

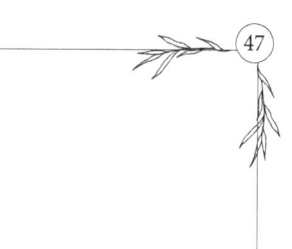

No Stone Unturned

Alone I stand my hat in hand looking down on fresh cut grass.
The stone I face with words I placed, of thoughts that I let pass.
The flowers laid upon the grave for her unplanned demise,
A late attempt they represent, as tears drop from my eyes.

Thoughts so blind my stubborn mind too proud to reveal,
The truth within to my chagrin there's no court for appeal.
I remember when the time was then, now how can I forget,
Will years forgive the gloom I live and soothe the cold regret?

My fuzzy eyes begin to rise I turn and look to see,
The nightmare gone now she lives on resting peaceful next to me.
The lingered fear could reappear but now that I have learned,
My words expressed each day I'm blessed I'll leave no stone unturned.

No stone unturned perhaps I've learned her presence I revere.
Now when I speak the words I seek are chosen to endear.
And we will know if one must go the other left back will grieve but then
The love so told will not grow old, saved for when we meet again.

Dennis Corcoran

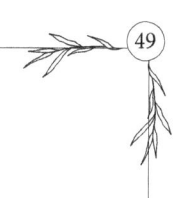

The Paddler

Shoving off the sand to water patterned ripples veer,
My vessel bobs and settles into liquid crystal clear.
The paddle slaps the surface dipping for a stroke,
Blazing through the lily pads I hear the bullfrog croak.

Reaching, pulling, guiding, pointed to the breeze,
The birds begin to chirp flying high above the trees.
Tiny waves approach my bow ringing pitter–patter,
Gliding through the silky lake while nothing seems to matter.

The surface breaks a fish appears flipping in the air,
The seagull dives and hits the mark, the fish becomes her fare.
The sounds I hear are live and real, the sights I see not fake,
This nature feeds my hunger, to paddle 'cross the lake.

Looking back from where I came,
Something doesn't feel the same.
The wind picked up and changed its' course,
Now facing me with quite a force.

No choice now, just paddle through,
A struggle, not much I could do.
With vigor to the other side,
Of course, that's when the gale wind died.

Dennis Corcoran

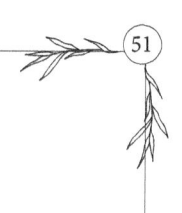

The Right Branch

Of course it starts at the bottom,
Looking up at a towering loaded tree.
Loaded with far reaching blooming branches,
Begging to be climbed.

The first challenge is a big one.
The lowest branch is almost out of reach.
It takes a stretch, at least.
Let's give it a shot.

Standing tall with arms extended,
My fingers wrap tightly around the branch.
Pulling upward I swing my legs over to the trunk of the tree.
Hanging from the branch with my feet planted on the trunk, I
walk upwards.

I swing my leg over the top of the branch.
Now I can pull myself up to straddle it.
Overhead are so many random limbs,
Enough, I think, to get me to the top.

A branch on the opposite side is reachable.
It seems to be the best option for my next step.
I step, and reach for a limb above that one.
It is thick enough to support my weight.

That worked out well.
And so it goes. I work my way up.
Instincts and common sense tell me when to stop.
I have climbed as high as possible.

Biophilia: Nature and Human Nature

One more step could risk tragedy.
A broken branch would have extreme consequences.
An abrupt decline, bouncing off limbs,
Would surely result in a catastrophic ending.

But I don't think about that.
I begin my descent,
Knowing I need to be home for dinner soon.
Mother would worry.

Dennis Corcoran

Dennis Corcoran

Skipping Stones

Wandering solely along in the soft sand,
The ocean to my side barely moved.
The air surrounding me was still.
The warmth of the sun pressed gently against my skin.
It was that kind of day, and I was happy to be a part of it.

Tranquil thoughts passed through my mind.
Not pondering, just peaceful.
My body moved graciously and with ease,
Serenity blending with each step.
Beholden to the earth I walked upon.

I could look up to the sky, or out to the sea,
Or simply look down to the sand.
Natures treasures to gaze upon.
A seagull spreading its wings,
A Hermit crab scurrying along.

Or a stone in the sand.
So many of them, each unique.
Some too large to be called a stone.
Some the size of a pebble.
And the millions of tiny grains that made up the sand.

My eyes feasted upon one particular stone.
The thought occurred to me.
This stone was special.
Flat, smooth, round and just the right size.
This was my skipping stone.

I anxiously picked up the perfect stone.
Walking to water's edge, I positioned it in my hand.
Bringing my arm back to a sidearm throwing position,
I hurled the stone as level as I could to the water.
The perfect stone skipped more times than I could count.

Biophilia: Nature and Human Nature

No one there to see, just me.
But I knew this was one of the best skipping stones ever.
And I had hurled the stone perfectly.
That was all I needed for now.
It was that kind of day, and I was happy to be a part of it.

Dennis Corcoran

Dennis Corcoran

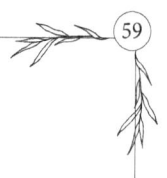

That Song

To describe it is not feasible.
If you try, you will stumble with a lack of authenticity.

Words don't translate…
Unless words are put to music.
The same is true with instruments.
The guitar stands, longing to be picked in such a way.
The piano sits so grand, waiting for talented fingers to tap the keys.
Add a vocalist with words that flow, and a song is born.

As defined, Music is vocals or instrumental sounds,
Singularly or combined in such a way,
As to produce beauty of form, harmony,
And expressions of emotion.

So blessed are those that have the talent to produce it.
So blessed we are if we have the sense to hear it.

I once heard a song that moved me so,
I unknowingly started to hum along,
When I paused for a second and looked below.
My foot was tapping to the beat of that song.

That song became so special to me,
I played it over and over again.
20 years later, or more it could be,
That song still plays from way back when.

I still hum and tap my foot when it plays,
Even after all of these years.
So special, it will live beyond my days,
That mystical, musical song to my ears.

Dennis Corcoran

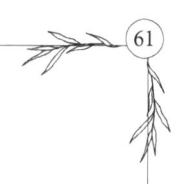

This Old Boat

This old boat it shows my years,
And how I've come to know.
That loyalty will squash one's fears,
No matter how the wind will blow.

The waves that thrash against her bow,
Are no match for her sailing pride.
She struggles but pulls through somehow,
The rock and roll she takes in stride.

One night searching for my port I felt,
My days ahead were through.
The wind and fog and rain had dealt,
A wave too big, the engine blew.

We drifted as I fought the wheel,
Aimless was our flight.
Steering was a hopeless deal,
But she held up throughout the night.

When morning came upon a reef,
I found us to be lodged.
The storm had passed and my belief,
A bullet we had dodged

I patched her up soon after that,
And you may wonder why.
Like nine lives from an old tomcat,
This old boat would never die.

Biophilia: Nature and Human Nature

Dennis Corcoran

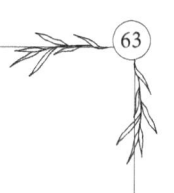

Tick Tock

Tick tock, look at the clock, same as yesterday,
Tick Tock, look at the clock, our world is in delay.
Paused, like a calm in a stormy sea,
Surviving this pandemic mystery.

So I stay at home thinking, all day long,
With my mind, such a powerful tool,
Wondering what to make of it all,
Isolated, except for my thoughts.

And my thoughts wander through life.
My Mother, my father, my sisters, my brother,
My children my friends, all those I have loved.
All that I have done or not done, wishing I had.

The places I have been, the places I want to go,
The things I want to say, or wish that I had said.
And then, the thought of whom I want to be,
Or who I am, because I have lived.

For those who know me for who I think I am,
And see the person I have wanted to be,
I know you too. I have witnessed your presence.
That is our concrete bond in life.

Tick Tock, look at the clock, same as tomorrow,
Tick tock, look at the clock, our world is here to borrow.
And when it's time to give it back, sad as it may be,
I'll see you in the heavens, there for you and me.

Biophilia: Nature and Human Nature

Dennis Corcoran

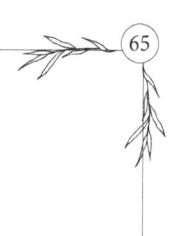

Too Late For Luck

Luck, seldom surfacing in my name.
Good fortune lacking, same old same.
Wisdom points to one's self for blame.
For one waiting, luck never came.

Slacking, waiting, one person found,
The wise man wrong, fate came around.
Good fortune landed, aimlessly bound,
Finding its target, one making no sound.

Not for me, searching, hoping for some,
Looking for more where that fortune came from.
Seeking in vain for this good luck to come,
Finding no luck, not even a crumb.

Nine times in ten, odds pointing my way,
This one without luck is where I will stay.
For as luck would have it I decided to play,
And my number came up on my dying day.

Dennis Corcoran

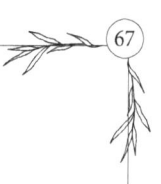

Twin Towers

I remember looking up one day,
A building oh so high.
It's mirror image on display,
Twin towers in the sky.

An image that we all knew well,
A symbol of our working pride.
Until the day the towers fell,
From evil on the other side.

Now it's time to start again,
No matter what the cost.
To learn, rebuild, do what we can,
In memory of the ones we lost.

And when all is said and done,
Our States United through and through,
Our freedom, like the rising sun,
Still here for you and me.

United we will always stand
Even in our darkest hours.
The spirit of the freest land
Will resurrect the old twin towers.

History will no doubt reveal that those who lost their lives on the tragic day of September 11, 2001 served to ignite the will of our people to commence a mission to ensure our society remains strong and harmonious in a peaceful existence, much in the same way past generations of Americans have stood their ground fighting victoriously to preserve the principles our great country was built on.

Biophilia: Nature and Human Nature

Dennis Corcoran

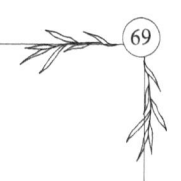

While You Were Away

While you were away,
the sun still glimmered on the river below.
Rippling waves bounced specks of light
that piqued my point of view.
Leaves so green from trees so tall
blended with brilliance,
from that magnificent sun above.

The moon crept up silently,
forming shadows that replaced the receding radiance.
A few twinkling stars appeared,
reminding me of eternity, so hard to define.
Sleep approached, dreams followed.

Once again, the sun showed up
to remind me of a new day.
The new one began like the last one,
with all of nature's wonders back again.
So fortunate for me, from my vantage point.

All of this, while you were away.
But in my mind was a constant reminder.
It kept telling me it's even better than this.
In my mind was a picture of you.
What I thought about most,
While you were away.

Biophilia: Nature and Human Nature

Dennis Corcoran

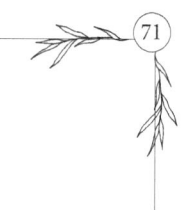

A Word To The Wise

Adult time… It's different than children's time.
Passing by abruptly as the future comes quicker.
Birthdays come and go with the blink of an eye.
There are so many from the past.
Too soon, there are less in the future. Who can tell?

A child looks forward to their next birthday. It takes forever.
They've only had a few to remember.
To compensate for the long wait, we let them count half years.
A child has their life ahead of them.

Child time looks at how great it will be.
Adult time knows what it was like back then.
Child time looks at the future to see,
And then they're adults, remembering when.

The time is the same for the young and old.
The world still spins at its natural pace.
A word to the wise, like we've often been told.
Slow down, take your time, this is no race.

www.ingramcontent.com/pod-product-compliance
Lightning Source LLC
Chambersburg PA
CBHW051645120626
46551CB00015B/2219